development of sound character. Our hope is that this book can be used to instill seeds of truth into very young minds.

Photo Credits
Corel Corporation: Front and back cover, 2, 4, 7, 9, 10, 12 (bottom), 13, 14, 15, 16 (bottom), 17, 19, 20 (bottom), 21 (top), 22, 24
PhotoDisc: 3, 6, 8, 18, 20 (top)
Adobe: 5 (bottom)
Gerry Ellis/Just Animals by Digital Vision/ Getty Images: 12 (top), 23

Copyright, 2011
by
Rod and Staff Publishers, Inc.
P.O. Box 3, Hwy. 172
Crockett, Kentucky 41413

Telephone: 606-522-4348

Printed in U.S.A.

ISBN 978-07399-2427-3

Catalog no. 2896

3 4 5 6 7 — 25 24 23 22 20 19 18 17 16

Leopard

Mountain Goat

Baby Mountain Goat

Tiger

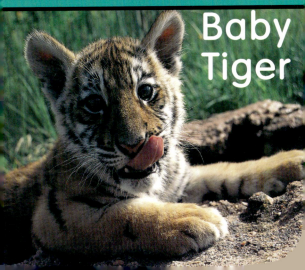
Baby Tiger

Black Bear

Polar Bear

Fox

Baby Bear

Dolphin

Seal Pup

Ostrich

Tortoise

Wolf

Zebra

Monkey

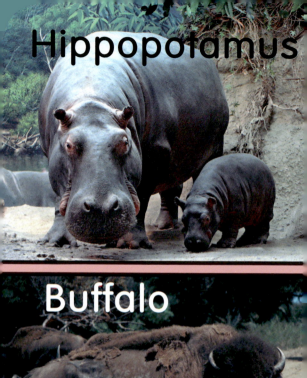

Hippopotamus

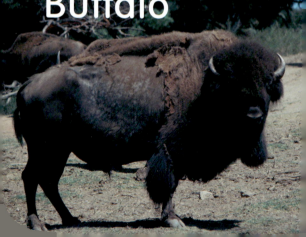

Buffalo

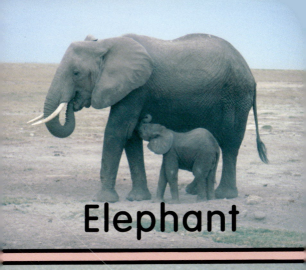
Elephant

Camel

Elephant

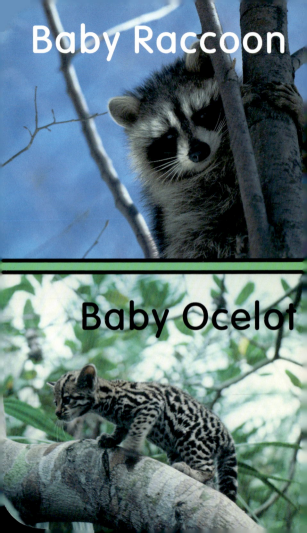

Kangaroo

Lion

Jaguar